HAG DANCES

HAG DANCES

Susan Wismer

AT BAY press

WINNIPEG

Hag Dances

Design and layout by Lucas c Pauls and M. C. Joudrey.

Published by At Bay Press May 2025.

Library and Archives Canada cataloguing in publication is available upon request.

ISBN 978-1-998779-68-0

Printed and bound in Canada.

FSC www.fsc.org MIX Paper | Supporting responsible forestry FSC® C016245

This book is printed on acid free paper that is 100% recycled ancient forest friendly (100% post-consumer recycled).

First Edition

10 9 8 7 6 5 4 3 2 1

atbaypress.com

Funded by the Government of Canada | Canada

Canada Council for the Arts Conseil des arts du Canada

We acknowledge the support of the Canada Council for the Arts.

MANITOBA ARTS COUNCIL CONSEIL DES ARTS DU MANITOBA

With the generous support of the Manitoba Arts Council.

HAG DANCES

FIRST WORDS: A DEDICATION

These poems were written on the shorelines of Manidoo-zaaga'igan (Georgian Bay) in Ontario. I live on Treaty 18 territory, currently under the stewardship of the Saugeen Ojibway Nation and the Three Fires Confederacy. My ancestors arrived in what is now Canada about 200 years ago looking for refuge. I am grateful for the life I have and I regret deeply colonization's harms to the land and its Indigenous peoples. In the interests of all my relations and their descendants, I dedicate myself to this Earth and its unconditional embrace. In that spirit, I offer these poems.

HAND SHADOWS

SINCE I AM STILL HERE

How will I move through this time before?

Ruffed grouse, strawberries, the tall leaning spruce tree
across the back fence – constant
rhythmic, drumming,
below and above, fire
Earth's centre, heat of the sun

Crab apples hang frozen on the tree through winter,
with each storm, frost and thaw they soften, become
food for robins and a cedar waxwing

I still have so much to learn

Wonder and desire hold me here, and of course

gravity

BEFORE

Summer wind through lavender's dusked leaves
garden gate boards weathered grey
the house finch's long song soars
from crab apple tree branches

dark nimbus clouds scud
swift off the lake before
thunder and rain
send us running
to garden tools
laundry lines
windows

holding
your hands cupped in mine
your knuckles blue-veined
small knobs of arthritis
at the joints of two fingers

a breath –
                our clasped palms

AURORA BOREALIS

Celestial
        falling

through stellar obsidian skies   we were
        arms flung   faces raised
                mouths filled with wind

whirling
high over trees

shape-shifted creatures of night fired light
raven black wings   silver manes

        sharp shining hooves

Returned   we were
almost too late

to remember

we are humans

                descendant

                        from stars

HAND SHADOWS

Imprisoned
bound hands, cuffed wrists
fingers clenched and outstretched
clenched again

The bagpipe's nine notes
hearken the possible –
breathe through the keen cuts
of grief, sun silent stripes
the barred window
on the wall her fingers draw
chiaroscuro
shadow and light

her butterflies fly

SANCTUARY

Nettles, scotch thistle, dame's rocket, chickweed
wild lettuce, blue clouds of forget-me-not
all unkempt in my garden

sun stencilled sumac, warm scent
of lilac, loamed shade under maples
                    one toad

My trowel furrows, digs deep
in this life I fear, world peace
will not come

Regardless unasked
the wood fern
uncurls

FORECAST

The scent on this morning's wind is of rain
but I'll hang wet laundry out anyway
pinning up hope for good weather, again.
Not much else to say to you today –
a black squirrel hops along the back fence,
Big Dog growls, barks, runs fast, knowing
he hasn't got even the tiniest chance,
never comes close to catching
a squirrel. But each day he'll try
for the miraculous impossible
as will I, as will I –

I'll pray to stop the unstoppable,
peg out clothes in the wind while it rains

Shout out *Please don't die,* and shout out again

MOMENTS

The second time the dog scratches at the door
I guess he really does want out

but I let him whine for a moment while sirens wail
into my ear from a few blocks away

one long breath catches my throat, wooden
spoon in my hand, a pause from stirring
ginger and garlic in pumpkin soup

waiting at the door
for the dog to return,
wondering

when it first started, my thought –
you
will go

This morning I kneel in the garden to see
        if our peas have come through the night

hear blue jays send familiar gate-creaking calls
        from the dying ash tree

turn slowly back to the house, uncertain
        how to return

to the gape of your hard-pressed gasping
        the rapid uneven beat of your pulse

still hoping we haven't
        run out
        of time

SILENCE

Near the end of the lane the sentinel stands,
two fallen gashed limbs prostrate on earth

Ephemera: hepatica, toad lily, trillium, rue
springtime-gone, my feet walking by

Moon shine, hoarfrost, a red fox slips past into trees
behind there are child shadows haunting

Hunters are out there, it's autumn
distant gun blasts, snow coming soon

Above fallen branches, this hollow trunk gathers
me, homes me in silence

HOURGLASS

Sand drifts through
the narrowed waist
of my dreaming

mirrored, our bodies
unfurl, blurred, blended,
                    softened

time is steadfast, falling
a long coil of red ribbon unspools
reflection, glass walls –
what might have been

fine-grained, passing, beloved
the dusting of years

STILL THE MOON

Still the moon rises *as if* content
gibbous, waxing, untouched by the world
as it is, half-hidden face, distant

so much withheld: touch has gone absent
the earth spins wild unbearable nights, turns
still, the moon rises almost content

a white swan on her nest, curled constant
close, the beach, safe and calm, one eye
gleams light, a half-hidden face, distant

you note every day's endless extent
in the city where people are dying
still the moon rises, as if content
with your absence

eight wearied weeks spent
away, are you well: audio fades
video blurs, half-hidden face, distant

each day now we say, *soon but not yet...*
the unbearable absence of touch
still the moon rises as if content
where you are, half-hidden face, distant

NIGHT VISION

Underfoot, autumn-dry leaves crumble, whisper
under three stars, white bands of cloud,
                                        haloed moon

draws down a path while the dark cabin waits
tonight's air is uncommonly warm

I open the green-painted door, light candles,
rekindle the fire, will soon sleep

tree hands reach naked
through moon's falling light

their prayers constant, implacable, rising

AUTUMN AUBADE

Geese fly south, summer
tucked under their wings

October's last dawn
comes in frostlight
grey dreams and I am
here beside you

as late flight, sunlight
stealing away

DRESDEN CUP

Poland 1943

Found
by the roadside
three cups and three saucers

spare beauties of smooth rounded shape
some hesitant hand
brushed paint over porcelain
blue rise of line along curve across lip

horns of a ram
fern tendrils unfurling in spring
curls on the neck
of her young daughter's head

She carried these with her
all through that war
scalpel and morphine
her doctor-hands bloodied
sirens Red Cross tents
ambulance bombs

her children in Canada
so little could be kept

safe

England 1945

What endures is by chance
the fragile-made-sacred
by circumstance
                    three saucers
                three cups

Canada 2025

I want

hot black tea, this Dresden cup
warm in my hands, steam pearling the air

        to imagine the artist

lift cup to the light
        tip brush to paint
            place one final dot
                below each tender curl

STORIES

What toes have to say
about wings, about angels
daring to ask –

all that a face holds
untold, rising
wordless as feathers
to carry

outstretched foot, arms reaching
quiet face, your crooked elbow
raised – a practice
of flying

stories, stories
still heard

    when the drummers go home
    when the dancers are gone

in the soft smudge of feet
on the floor

AFTER ALL

The bow scrapes
across strings, cello's body
resonates, sings, breathes
in my arms

Under your pianist hands, keys
white, black rise and fall
that slight, graceful lift
of your head, our eyes
catching light –
memory

All those songs
we sang and sang
are with me still

but I'm fine
after all
without you

MAY FALLS INTO JUNE

for Don

My brother, you have our mother's brown eyes,
the sky is inside, colours of clam shell,
a tube down your throat, you are ill

lost behind clouds, dawn's slender light rises
mist in the pine trees, trout lilies in bloom
yellow heads bow at my feet

ICU says it all, white-grey days slip to
weeks feel like months, hope pulls
fierce frantic, a snarling chained dog –

from sun-rested clouds
blackbirds sing in your voice, search
green treetops for you

under blue tender skies, I bend
toward earth, lift out weeds,
lay them down –

I cannot remember what I once knew

May falls into June, cell phone in my pocket,
hospital on speed dial, black flies bite my neck,
sun reddens my arms, lilac blooms fade

I sit by your bed, stroke your silent hand,
screens flash blue and red, wave yellow lines
light gallops forward

You are still here

COMING HOME

How to prepare for whatever will come
with the seasons? Last summer was breathless
a great maw beside me through too many weeks
of sitting by you and your hospital bed

Pneumonia a ravening beast wanting
to take you away, then just as it came
without warning or hope, illness
lumbered away

We went camping. Each tree-shadowed
morning, our awkward crawl from the tent,
contralto tent zippers in tune with the campfire
hiss of damp wood. Sunrise a fish, salmon
and gold, slides into the lake

For cold hands, hot tea. A healing
of ground squirrels, capering comics
with green pinecone cigars in their mouths
cheroot back and forth

I want to stay
with the loons and the mist
but we have to come home
to autumn

Tonight cool air flows through
cracked-open windows, my body curls
round your warmth, the long nobbled line
of your spine, worn quilt is a comfort
holding me

I gather myself close around you sleepless
needing to listen, to be sure
you are breathing

I THOUGHT I HAD MORE TIME

Snow came this year swiftly
thick folds over unraked leaves
white piles fill my garden chairs

Today more snow:
I shovel the walk while
in paper bags, tulip bulbs wait

Taken by surprise, the garden hose
stands frozen in curves

Maybe this will all melt:
I'll rake snow-sodden leaves
onto turned vegetable beds, trowel
my way through frost-crusted earth
plant bulbs in deep holes with a little blood meal
to discourage the squirrels

I carry the hose to the basement,
stack garden chairs under eaves,
pile flowerpots upside down
until spring   I thought
I had more time

ONE BLUE THREAD

PERFECTION

Every small radish is
an earthbound globe,
unseen adventurer in the underland
welcoming this spring's raised bed –

moist soil *friable,* worms' reach, tender
delicate root threads grow, stretch
                                        descend

Are we too careful with courage
with joy?

To keep each small living creature
intact, naked, fearless: two heart-shaped leaves
breathe a hint of red bulb, white rootlets net,
cluster in the cup of one hand

seedlings a tangle in slow explorations
thinned, moistened, separate
return to waiting soil

In the welcoming breath
of this only day

a promise of
rain, mist brushes cool
on my sleep-warmed cheeks, ferns push
tight curls out of earth, becoming

Are we too careless with what falters,
with loss?

my weary hands plunge into dirt,
fingertips probe cautious, touch tendrils,
new shoots, every springtime's returns

in the morning, perfection – small plants,
damp soil
and radishes

SHED

Solitude: open field, no driveway, no lane
among tall meadow grasses, green and golden heads
brush once-white clapboard sides feathered grey

Sturdy sheet metal roof, wind-weathered strength of wide
doors long closed, hinges rough, rusted, flaking

Big wooden hen squats low in her field,
clucks over mouse nests, cobwebs, dark secrets –
worm legions wiggle below her earth floor
one bale of hay lies moulding,
forgotten

She is a shape-shifter, camouflaged spy,
trusted, she sends underground messages via
mycelia from gnarled apple trees
by one lonely elm to sugar maples, red pines,
the far stand of red cedars cloistered, ancient

Shed's wood planks remember
how to creak with the winds, how to work for
the trees, she wants them to prevail

WHEN I THINK OF THAT AUTUMN

As purposeful sorrows, insistence on fire
frost hurricanes plague, inexorable losses
of light every day, the garden reluctant
her last few green beans gone swollen and rusty,
my supplicant hands rush nightly to gather
old bedsheets, cover tomatoes,
keep basil safe from frost

I consider mycelium's underground weaving,
fungal-thrust forward through soil into fairy ring
toadstools and white puffball moons
soft-skinned and turning, in
the wisdom of spores, soon
back into earth.

GENESIS

We arrived there and found the soil was
not good: sparse cover on straggled patches
of Kentucky Blue grass poor, unsuited
to the climes of this place, underneath
cinders, gravel, rocks
untilled hard clay

Old trampled Shed Bed, I called it –
Runaway Rascally Seed Burglar, Root-Wrangler
Never-Flower, Carrot-Hater, Pole Bean Toppler –
                    how unkind I was, and impatient

We composted kitchen waste,
poached leaf bags from neighbours,
raked every gleaned leaf
onto our hard-bitten yard

So much to ask of buried history
and of the name
we could finally give it –

                    Our Garden

UMBRELLA

Umbrella fly sky
look up see ribs
stretched windy flap wet
battered cloth black
grip shaft
handle
crook

under hover
stand cover
hold on rain
drops will
fall

wind-blast snap off
shield gust side in
side out fly topsy
down turvy
away

crow feather cloud
flap black bird flock
broken rib busted
open happy
hands
wide

let
go let
fly

ILLUMINATION

How many centuries of being pressed down
does it take to turn sandstone to light, to bring it
to rest in the warm cushioned palm of my hand?

Pebble, white quartz barely thumb-sized, rounded
by stories of journeys through waters – what
ancient rivers, glaciers, tropical seas?

Shining and limned with traces of grey and
red granite, black tourmaline in pockmarks
where pyrite or chert once fell away

All this small rock knows about lasting,
to have come from the earth, to be with it now
a glimmering

TODAY I BECOME

Shadows pass in a mirror, fleeting
a darkness, pearl-grey light, early day

unforeseen rain falls on this too-mild winter
morning's harbinger of ice, slick roads

in the kitchen, an orange peel pulls away slowly
one long graceful spiral drops into a metal bucket

compost for the backyard pile, welcomed
by mice who tunnel, warm there through winter

smooth brown flanks, skittered back feet, quick
flash of white furred belly, naked tail

each small thing I see

ONE BLUE THREAD

Old Poet knows
she is dropped leaves,
wanting winter's light touch
on her knots, her stiff elbows,
the lowering bends
of her branches

when they call,
Come, sit here at the table,
come eat,
she replies,
I am the sound of tree bark's slow growing,
above me at night, stars weep leafless light.
I am footprints of camels, unseen by the wind.
Inside solitude's desert tent, naked hands
weave me. I am one blue wool thread
in the rug at your feet.

SPIRITS

My ancestors are made of madness:
Cape Breton Strathspeys, evictions –
Fuadaichean nan Gàidhea – Highland Clearances
secrets, resentment, red hair

My ancestors appear in bagpipes, old rubber boots,
dance on worn kitchen floors, language lilts
shadows, ghost Gaelic traces lift
off my flat English tongue

Dairy cows, sea air, two pigs, burnt houses,
black-faced sheep, croft homes
abandoned, all left behind

What they could take when they left
to pass down –
                              my stubborn Scottish pride

INVOCATION

Black shawl scry mutter
stone spellbag herbs potions
boil iron cauldron –

I am bent-fired on broomstick
in cackling flight
through obsidian nights

Hecate come! Wander with me
over streets slivered ivory
by strawberry moons
call, listen, wail,
fly, walk, cast a spell

With each step and howl
hear my walking stick thump!
Hear me beat, beat away
at the imperilled heart
of the Anthropocene.

ADVICE

Remember Vasalisa, lost . . .
she found Baba Yaga's forest house
dancing on
wild chicken feet,
fearsome old woman
who would eat you alive, unless

you complete the impossible task

while she sleeps
crawl silent in darkness on
planked wooden floors
your blind fingers stroke each
splintered groove, seek
every cranny, gather each seed –

There's a doll in your pocket
She knows the way home.

MOTHER'S EVENING DANCE

One hand holds
the small silver opening
up to the light

Black thread measured nose-tip to
arm-stretch, three quick turns around
forefinger, roll of a thumb makes a knot,
chestnut curls at the back of her neck, jump
to the snap of snipping front teeth,
lips and tongue moisten one end before,
deft, she slips in the thread, on it a trace
of red lip-sticked lips, Revlon – *Fire and Ice*

Under the lamp
small lifts and falls
hand shadows

On her lap, fabric – cut, patch,
stitch, green, yellow, brown, tomato
pin cushion, lamplit moving thread, shining
needle dips and returns through worn elbows,
gaped knees, ripped sleeves gone unseamed,
    until weary from gathering all that is torn
    into her hands, she stands and turns
            leaves what remains unrepaired
                                for tomorrow

            Her arm's upward bend,
                      reach of her hand, twist
                       of a wrist, the lamp switch's

                                click
                                        darkened room

SPONTANEOUS COMBUSTION

Half-naked above me in autumn, the flowering crab
now laden with hard little apples –
the bites I take bitter
in my throat. Birds will ignore them
all winter long until frost
makes them softer and all
else is gone

from far away, the not-quite sound of your voice
ghosts my ears, colours fade, a familiar scent rises
worn soft with years, wind-dried cotton, the red quilt
you made for my bed, crab apple shades patchworked
red, pink, green, soft brown, off-white
thinned comfort for my questing

chilled fingers thrust bare garden
hands deep in fresh shards of bright new-cut
wood chips piled by the roots of the hard-appled
old tree, feel smoulder, find smoke
touch warmth, surprise
stinging the air, burning
tears in my eyes

water, air, matter, flesh
bone, breath, blood –
ignite

every conversation with my mother
        fire
                    at its heart

A PHOTOGRAPHER VISITS THE NURSING HOME

Hilda:

It's my hands that
your camera should
catch. Just like this,
here in my lap.

Hurry up now.
Before I change my mind.

Ruth:

I like myself best from the back –
I always have. I want
to be looking away.

Somewhere out there.
Some place that says,
Come. You come too.

Barbara:

Take that wooden chair. Put it under the tree.

I'm going to wear this white bedsheet.
Best use it's had, I dare say.
Let's drape it like this –
Can you tuck it in there?

Here's what you'll see:
the white sheet and my collarbones
shoulders and arms, dappled tree shadows,
sun on my face.

I want them to see me.

There's beauty in this, don't you know?

MOTHER'S DAY: A Daughter's Palinode

I take it all back, Mom –
every thought I ever had
that started with
    you should, or
    why can't you just

walk more by the ocean,
call up a friend, go
to Tai Chi, clean
that place up

quit morphine,
mindpower through pain,
do something

for you
just this once

of course, I meant
me, do this for me –

tell that smug doctor
you've had enough
of her

drugs
that don't help

you claim not to notice
that stuff has ruined you

your kidneys, your gut, those
prescriptions for opioids,
prednisone, blood thinners,

      your liver
              your eyes

I take all that back –

I wanted to kill
that doctor (still do)
even though we both knew
it was all too late

     and you
                          liked her

In those days
it took nothing
to crack your ribs, break
your holed, porous osteoarthritic
bones, just lift a teacup,
one surgeon said

You said, *Nothing*
to be done, just lie on the couch,
hope by tomorrow
the pain will be less

Mom, it's all far too late
but if I could, I would take it back

So selfish
I was then. At last
I have learned to know
nothing –
    no anger, no pain, no love
    and no hate could
    hold you here

From the day I was born
    something was coming
        to take you
            from me

HOW TO REMEMBER

After I kissed her forehead
squeezed her hand, said
I'll be back soon, Mom

what she said
could have been
    It's alright, dear, or
    Now, I need to rest, or

    Good-bye. . ..

Today I wrote a list:
bananas
hand cream
kombucha

PENTIMENTO

Red cedar, afternoon rain, an unbroken oyster shell
good for a soap dish, gnarled twist of driftwood
scent of my mother, two smooth grey branches
knot like an eye

Clouds on the mountain again –
oil pastels laid down, layer upon layer
Mount Baker's tip barely
comes through

The ferry shakes, trembles, heaves from the shore,
On the railing, blue veins, knob joints,
index finger turns in, my own hand becoming
heron's claw, hers

In my suitcase one painting, red scarf
her blue bowl

GRANDMOTHER

Day wanders backward
through mountains past
set crescent moon
gone unearthly to howl
as if wolf

marten deer rabbit
sky-born run wisped
under clouds hunting
or haunted am I
                    lost

in time's shape –
shifting turned home –
spun cobwebbed and
footworn to trenchant
star-bellied orb weaver
vole-rustled grasses
dust motes flick glint
round silk-threaded sun

here among saplings
riven oak bark old tree
hollowed out
heartwood deep-creviced
verdant crowned face

DON'T KNOW

Why I leave my shoes at your door   don't know
how to stop, though you tell me
        don't bother
                it's my mother's voice louder
                        her ghostly embrace
                stronger than all present moments

truth is   the house
I was raised in   always a mess
    but she taught me to love   my own unshod foot
                    bare on wood floors

don't know why that stays with me   when so much
                is gone

today the pink poppies
        paddywhacked bobbleheads   heave in
                        wind and rain
wild waving tall silver-furred stalks
                thin fringed pink petals
                    holding on

must be hard   but *they* keep their heads on
keep themselves together, just can't help wishing

my own soft body was that strong

don't know how
to begin
to stop seeing
all that's gone wrong
so far today
if I turn
off my cellphone you can't call me and

and I want you to know
that I'm here

A CROWN FOR THE KITCHEN

REDHEADED SPATULA

A hand-held bend, a dance of twisted wrist,
our dervish turns, redhead whirling among
solemn spoons, wood-handled knives, wired whisk –
scavenger, scrimper, lover of leaving
no trace behind. Consummate, her circling
is swift, deft, mark-less, bright silicone scrape
of blade on bowl, dear Kitchen friend bringing
me gifts – good bits that Spoon and Whisk don't take,
lifts up what they would abandon and then
with a bow to Pot and Pan, turns to offer
teasers for my tongue. Like red currant jam,
she leaves me with a taste that lingers for
spatulated morsels she extracts
in joyful obligation to her task.

BROWN BETTY TEAPOT

In joyful obligation to her task,
Teapot waits to hear the keening cry of
Kettle's whistled steam, her slow refract
fears none of water's heat or scalding boils
nor Kettle's ghostly moans and roiling spills.
Her mission is creation: brew and steep
tea's high-grown leaves from terraced hills.
Misted, musky, warm, she holds the scents
of sun and rain from far-off storied places –
Oolong, Lapsang Souchong, Yunnan, Assam –
Teapot is simple strength of stoneware, grace
for a perfect cup, her round-bellied warmth
presides at home with comfort, quiet, calm
while life arrives, holds us, pours out. Goes on.

SAUCEPAN

Life arrives, holds us, turns, leaves, goes on –
like Saucepan disappearing after years
of daily use. Copper mottled bottom
greened, handle loose from all the heft and heat
of favourite foods: morning's fragrant oatmeal,
lunchtime soups, yesterday's beef stew reheated,
his cupboard space looms vacant but lonely
Lid still lingers. Longing has us haunted –
Saucepan's loss weighs heavier each day
in our empty hands. Bamboo Spoon, bereft
of close companion, wonders, waits
calls out, *Where did you go, Saucepan, Old Pot?*
Strange, replies Spoon, *how Absence comes to stay* –
holds space, palpable, present, unnamed.

PINE TABLE

Holding space, palpable, present, named –
Pine Table's wooden legs, one well-gnawed
by Thumper's teeth one absent-minded day
while no one watched. Bunny twelve years gone,
runic indents pressed in wide pine boards –
children long grown now: Pine Table remains.
French dictées, math, Third Grade's misspelled words,
tears, anger, joy, secrets shared, whispered names
secrets untold, held in trust by wood below
an oft-washed cotton tablecloth, candles'
beeswax honeyed light, scent of sourdough,
hot soup, tulips in a glass jar. Pine Table
once tree, now home to memories and love –
knows what it is to gather. And to give.

KITCHEN WINDOW

To know what it is to gather, to give:
Through frosty glass, hungry chickadees,
early robins huddle in trees, shiver
and wait while I refill feeders with seed.
Snow blizzards the air, in March-iced days –
cars dodge past snowdrifts, slithering home.
In Window's light, warm Kitchen waits.
I heat up bean soup, make dinner alone,
watch candleflames flicker in drafts that slide
through sills, meanwhile in gale's blow and howl,
birds go to refuge and time slips untied
'til boots thump at the door and you're home now
snow-spackled hugs gust all worries away.
Kitchen Window sees it all, so clearly.

CORN BROOM

Corn Broom sees all, so clearly, so cleansing
corn-bristled wood-handled sweeper of tumbles
tow-bottomed seeker of unnoticed leavings –
whatever falls by spill, break or crumble,
Dust Pan and Broom help us gather it all.
After each of Big Dog's joy-filled escapes,
his tardy returns: dirty legs, wet muddy paws,
smelly smashed pumpkin all over his face –
after warm suds, scrub brush and towels,
Dog dried and clean, it's Dust Pan and Broom,
their full rhythmic *swish,* from corners to walls,
always Corn Broom, a chanting clean sweep, psalms
for the Kitchen, for runbackhome Dog, daily songs.

CHIPPED CUP

Songs for the Kitchen, daily songs, night and morn,
Brown Betty Teapot waits, marling hot steam,
Silver Teaspoon beside her, tarnished and worn.
White Pitcher pours milk in Chipped Cup's black tea.
Pine Table's wood boards keeping time, hold us
all, as Teaspoon rings small bells and milk swirls
in Chipped Cup. I see Cup soon will leave us –
even now through her cracks tannic beads swell –
I fill Chipped Cup again now while I can,
knowing one day porcelain pieces will fall
to Broom's bristled care, while Spoon misses Pan
and Red-headed Spatula loves us, all.

In Window's light, Kitchen is always like this –
hand-held, bent, dancing, slight twist of wrist.

CAMINO

TRAVELS TO NEPAL

Turkey, 1972

At a small café in Istanbul,
a man old to me then, bought us wine
deep red and tannic, foreign to my tongue.
After hours of talk about travel, politics, life,
he walked with me through unlit late streets
to the youth hostel

Fatherly as my own father never was,
in plain speech from a mouth not easily tuned
to the rough-cobbled words of English,
he counseled

Do not go alone to Kathmandu

I, who had seen emptied eyes more than once
in young women travellers
listened, turned back

Ontario, 1987

Canada, home
Babies and laundry, I teach what I can
that will pay, plant apples and rhubarb
grow lettuce, radishes, compost, recycle,
walk children to school through waves
of fatigue, read bedtime stories

At the Guelph Public Library on the give-away table:
The Lonely Planet Guide to Nepal 1985. I carry
it home where it stays: a book labelled `Discard'
dreams wrapped in a silk scarf, tucked away
at the back of a drawer, promises of

Annapurna, Himalaya, Lalitpur, Pokhara
stupas and temples, saffron spices, yak butter tea,
long treks between tea houses. Unknown words,
whispered rituals, mountain nights

Ontario, 2025

My children are adults, the book left behind
but I want you to know
I'm still on my way to Nepal

EQUINOX DIARY

Light leans toward winter, angled for
home through neighbourhood streets –
a small park between parking lots, afternoon
sun slants gold in the creek. Leaves brown,
yellow, rust, spiral, fall

Light leans, catches red,
the painted wood bridge,
white-tasselled grasses,
Katano Friendship Garden

Vanished footprints, old friends'
memory hangs in pruned trees,
plumed grasses, high penny flute
notes, voices of children at play,
bringing red furred bobs of
sumac while we chatted and laughed
with our talk of small matters –
warm coats for winter, new boots
for winter, growing feet –

Kate and Pat, gone now from this garden,
this town, from each other

Light runs tendrils through my fingers
thinned gold in the blue grey descent of today,
robins and cardinals cluster, chilled
silent in pine branches above me,
I'm thinking of Kate, tomorrow
I'll call her – she has the children,
I hope Pat is well.

ANTIPHON UKRAINE, MARCH 2022

Telling, tolling
resounding, repeated
                    insistent

on dark wounds of earth
bloodied limbs marked refusing,
                    resistant, plangent

in singing, dance, stories
to listen,
                    remember
each silenced voice

over and under
the boom thrust of war
exploding every
               cold-hearted bomb

VIA RAIL ONE

What measures a life?
Fox tracks, red blood, white snow, bits of fur,
birches cluster together, companionable shelter
this train, passing

Settling in, you here beside me
Snow. Bright winter sun. Clouds.
Lake Superior, Manitoba prairie, Northern lights:
Canada, passing

This morning I ache:
left shoulder, stiff neck, right hip,
new constant pain? Or today's
simple discomforts, passing

Your warm sloping thigh,
our bodies just as they are –
acceptance, at last: a tenderness I once felt
only in passing –

Missed turns, unmarked paths,
retraced steps, unmet searching
earlier years had no slowing down. What did I
miss in bypassing?

This robust red glow, well-aged
in my hand, rounded and welcome –
Burgundy wine, slow sips on my tongue: evening
rolls on, passing

Slow motion; rhythmic rumbles,
click-clacks; whistlestops, sidings,
your hand in mine, sound of your voice. Cadence of
years, passing

Wordless wheels turning,
songs of our passages. Not always easy –
but here we are: two travellers in
landscapes, lifetimes, passing

CAMINO

After all that can't be undone

after warnings, apologies, too little too late,
wildfires, floods, viruses, war –

plagues still slouching among us

three friends die of cancers in one month
and so much of what I fear
has already happened

how to find words

NO CEASEFIRE YET:
A Sijo for the Children

Daffodils raise yellow heads: they don't mind
harsh April's cold, wind-borne needles of rain –
bright faces still lift, small suns that shine
at relentless grey mackerel skies. Just like them
my wide-open mouth shouts loud
even though

TWILIGHT AT RABANAL
Camino de Santiago

At the slip of day into night
through listening silence,
a riffle of pages unlined

black Pilot v7 pen cradled in quiet
homely comforts at the end
of another long day

foot-weary from walking –
on these smooth white pages
slight dark impress of ink

the chant of my coin's slotted fall,
low and metallic; warm scent
of spent wax, guttered rows

candleflame in the chapel,
these words my votives, brief
flicker, a match sings in your voice

solvitur ambulando
the way
    is found
        by walking

TIME

Burnished brown stones
on the trail, morning rain

In my backpack, a cell phone
stacks seconds, then minutes in
precarious towers, soon
fallen

I am already late –
never mind

Lean walking sticks
against smooth-skinned beech,
stoop to admire three stones:
the cup holding water,
a large-moulded round, small shard of
pink shines out
under gnarled roots

The forest gleams –

    All this before breakfast

IN THIS WASTE

Of emptied eye what cleaves is the wounding:
unyielding, blind-sided, swilled into the gutter
grim-gritted luster of encircled bared bone –

Ominous pearl of daily unseeing, ordinary
violence, unnoted. How to see
what is not

Amidst all winter's squanders, blustered March days,
mudded detritus tufts, sodden bits of black fur,
broken bone, gutted and ruined: dead squirrel

Looking down stepping over, walking by this
nobody – am I the wastrel
if I see no great loss?

For all you no-bodies –
    the wars and the woundings,
    out of my sight, gone from my gaze

Blessed art Thou among ghosts

REDSTART

(after Helen Humphreys, The Evening Chorus)

Song of the redstart begins

as melody
ends
in dissonance
comes

undone in the singing

WIND-BORN

Returned, I was no longer
        the same –

I took truth to be birds
                found wisdom in soil

                    saw woman wind-born
                            fall out of the sky

                            no longer a stranger

NORTH OF VERONA, CANOE LAKE ROAD

The sharp bleat of the fawn
when Don pushes it, trying to get it
to leave the road, the doe close by
in the woods, eyes on
the fawn, Don, the car . . .

The doe doesn't know
what to do. I can see
it must hurt her
to hear the fawn cry
so loud, so scared, the baby
just born and too young
to know the road
is a bad place to be.

When he gets back
into the car, Don drives away
so very slow, with such care.

He has fawn fur on his hands.

BECAUSE THE NEED IS

So great at four in the morning

wrapped up in blankets,
window flung wide
cold air pouring in

I am all listen,
all peer, searching

through misted darkness, for some
blacker blackness to come
swooshing past

Because the need is so great, it's enough

in this already shattered
and still-breaking
world

to hear
sung low, repeating
in perfect pitch, three clear notes

five beats of long pause –

awakened
by owls

WALK HOME

Night sounds
footsteps
behind
laughter breaking
glass voices
of men
    (Don't ever say
    'scared)'

Go feral
go nimble
grow swiftly
four paws
keen amber eyes
pointed ears
turned
toward
them

    (Say
    Nothing).

Loud voices
can often be
harmless

Be fierce
grab your phone
don't think
of running
breaking away
from
bitch, cutie, slut,
whore, honey,
hottie, ugly
old hag

Keep quiet
keep going
keep on
walking
home

PILGRIM

Dragonflies circle, eating blood-sucking bugs,
dogs are howling for bees, thumbnails scrape glass

Leaving the citadel, uncertain of safety,
vision clouded by cataracts, wars

Piety has no place here, only pilgrimage –
blindness is my guide in a world dense with smoke

Morning sun lights the garden while birds sleep –
all night it rained, liquid rushing through drainpipes

Outside the window a dragonfly circles:
What is life like with translucent wings?

NAME

I cannot remember

the last day
before

Gone
under hopeful
stories of maybe
perhaps not certain
used to be temporary
try idiopathic try
something try pills
please try again
later

Before
shame hope accept
listen at night in small
hours gone howl into
morning gone molten
crawl minutes burn
crucible pain
no escape

Under
how are you
gone with what's
wrong under where
does it hurt do you know
the word chronic what
do you call it is –
is there a
name

SIMPLICITY

A vast tenderness lies here
beyond forgiveness

in this generous and frightening wilderness

I live
embraced for this short time

my human body on this Earth
a simple offering

DONATIVO SEMPLICE

(after Oliver Schroer, *Ultreia*)

Padded brush of bare heels   toughened soles
sure of the ground   widespread toes
steps in the dance
arched fulcrum of feet on the floor

your arms as   winter   bare branches
lofted black into evening   fading cerulean sky
at the window
jade velvet curtains   shine in worn places

your hands a deft strength
I know each of your fingers by feel

slight inward turn of one distal joint
small hill of knuckle
slow rise of veins
deep blue touch of time   behind us ahead
earth's curve
encircles

Our bodies magnetic
in out our breaths are
pulse flying between us

and yet
what bars and grates
locked doors doorless halls windowless rooms
lie hidden here
in the high sheen of song

we are bent toward earth only to
rise run reach for air
lean against walls

clenched fists fall and fold

we are imprisoned
we have pieced our own cage

Black feathered crow three-legged oak stool
red ribbon unspooled on the floor
carved rosewood box scent of clove oil

A scallop shell we kept after Muxía
my mother's gold watch that will not keep
time, we are

our memories
flocked
murmurations birds
fly as if one
although each
has her own heart and wings –

What the mouth cannot say
the imprisoned heart still wingèd
remembers, sings

our bodies are bound
to return
unbidden
closer to earth –

my fingers trace whorls, inner folds of an ear
    deepened lines
round your mouth, the base of your neck

its delicate cup fits
    my tongue

your toes I have held in my hands, to my lips

How well our feet know the floor
    so much rests on that

heels turn   toes rise   callus-edged soles
    lift descend

my hand pressed to the curve of your spine

your wrist turned toward mine
    tender   we open   familiar

for this simple offering –

Beloved, you are my place of return

HAGEOGRAPHY

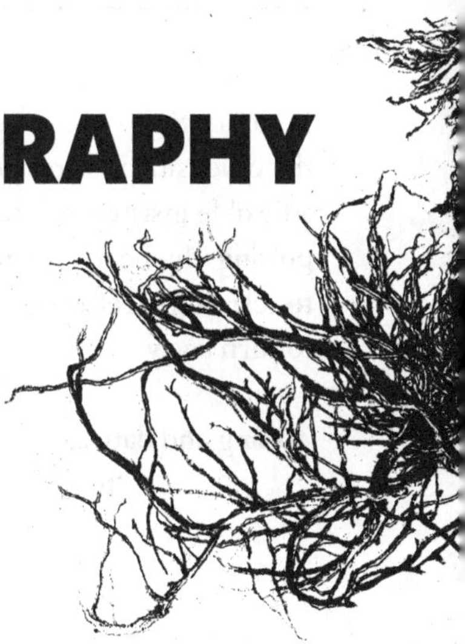

RESILIENCE

Is connection
the quiet sinew of resilience –
a flexible insistence   pulmonary
pulsing, the heart's commitment
to resistance, refusing
to turn away

To sing and dance,
                    to insist

THE PORCH

Milkweed nods, not yet in bloom.
On the porch small winds of morning
we sit in comfortable chairs, pens held
in gnarled fingers, white heads
bent over pages in
early summer sun

translucent the wings of our girlhoods / eyebrows
of our mothers / line-patterned webs
in the skin of our fingers / all our dead
lost
unborn

secrets of fingertips / toughened from cooking
fried onions
boiled potatoes / small scars
the inevitable burns
on our hands / rising
in early slant light
each unclaimed dream flickers
small fires hover on our knuckles

all that grief / all that love
sweet bitter strong / morning coffee / waking

red begonia, woolly lamb's ear
one outrageous white peony speaks
accents of green leaf, thick stem and root

a lone great blue heron
flies up from the pond
            water drops trail
        fall down
from
      sky
           seeking meadow.

at night we massage almond oil into stiff joints
trace blue lines across the back of each hand,
anoint the deepening cup
of each palm

thumb prints wear
after all these years of/ so much giving
                   words falling
                           into our hands

RITES OF SPRING

Shimmer and wave,
ash, maple, willow, pine –
a symphony of branches
leap, dip, flung allegro
by crescendo of winds –

Today it's all arias in minor keys
long vowels of loss turn around corners
winds beat at my windows
timpanic drumming

until relief, a quiet patter
pianissimo rain
before a new movement's clatter
of garbage lids, recycling bins rolling
down emptied streets, the *bang!*
of four boards flying
off the back fence

Underneath a faint drone
the overhead pulsing of wild geese
returning, and a friend
who stops by while trees
bow to the storm's lamentations
to ask a question
a question
big as the sky,

What would you give to stop war?

DUET FOR EVENING

Resonance of wood –
four hands, one piano
the body instrumental

a memory, long, softly played
  più piano, for what it is
  to be tree
    to transform

from slow beat of sap
pulsing *andante* through branches
singing of twigs, unfolding leaves

slender bending in harmony *dolce,*
our skilled fingers sweetly bridged over keys
well-practiced, accustomed to

sudden discord, mistakes, *ritardando*
of slowed passions, lost beats, hard
days of anger, old sorrows
changed tempos
rubato

through long years of return
to these bodies, resonant
instrumental our duet
four hands, one piano
from beginning to end

dal capo al fine

CANON FOR REHEARSAL

Wicking light
beneath piano, below drumbeats

a shadowed thrum
strong toes spread wide

supple feet of the dancers
grip broad umbered oak planks

gold bands of afternoon sun
glide, cross the floor

through tall windows lifted
hearing child voices, laughter

limestone church steeple
twin spired spines

contrapuntal

AT THE CROSSROADS

Cloaked in pale folds
of dark winter's coming
rock water sky
ice needled breath
leaves turn and fall
in slow-gyred swirls

She is dance to the glisten of sleet
frozen earth
keen skirl of hawk cries
chilled fingers grasp
evening's swift dropping

In her lantern's dying light
breathbeats
hauntsounds
her wailing –

a bain sidhe's touch

DECEMBER

Sun wants winter's rest
sleeps in 'til 8, off to bed by 6 –

this is December

Snow drifts over Earth
six-pointed wheels, white in blue air
cartwheeling angels

Candleflames stutter
frosty wind slides through my door
new light whistles up

I shovel the doorway
snow, snow, snow everywhere
wood fire, hot tea

Footprints of my snowshoes traced
around trees, mouse paw calligraphy
etched poems in snow

WOMAN SEEKS BODY

Convivial companion
pliant and kind not overly given
to pain. Strong steady
heart, generous hands

Piano player who loves
naked laughter, wide feet
curvy legs. Avid reader,
enjoys a hike, willing
to travel together
to ash, bone shards
compost:

offer what lasts
to calcium curves
of a snail shell, beach pebbles
gossamer

A STARKER FORM OF ART

I learn to love angles, sharp elbows,
Straighter lines in the shapes of my age.
Crescent moon crook, second finger, both hands

I attend to spiders, a funnelweaver
crawls on pale vellum, thinned skin
black and gold legs cross my arm,
afternoon in the garden

Tendons, ligaments, veins are
blue tattoos rising, I am
alive in the flesh of my own slow
dissolving, blurred lines through
my eveningtime eyes.

My body becomes a starker form
of art, it dances a gradual
descent toward Earth

CLIFF EDGE

One hand firm on dark earth
flat grass, the other hand hangs,
sends fingers
to touch

over the lip
they call *hag*

what remains
sunrise, lichen, tree trunk,
ghost of mountain, rounded
cheekbones

traced
contours, your face, my lips
our mouths, how they seek
open seawater, dark metal salt
for the tongue, volute
the shell of your ear
pearled
    singing

from the shimmering edge
of the world
    these last years

IN MY SKIN

> Stay is a sensitive word.
> we wear / who stayed
> and / who left
> in our skin forever.
> — Nayyirah Waheed, *Sojourn*

Our stories melt where sorrow surrounds
its own hard sweet centre, rough
edges. A pebble-broke tooth
and the tongue, their restless continual
rub, the inedible swallow
of long silences heard
from places where dreams
drained away   slipped off
and gone, just as I feared –
stay is a sensitive word

Barefoot we walked
our soles toughened on gravel
stone, dirt, stick, river, wind,
faces burnt with hot sun,
we wanted only what's real, to be
toe-stubbed on truth, unafraid –
naked shoulders were peeling
exposed, but still we were clothed
in all we had found / lost / betrayed –
wherever we go, we wear who stayed

My dirt-grimed hands, our purple –
bruised days, salted grit lining
my throat. Shadows surrounded me,
cupped both my eyes, fading scars
on the sole of one foot, portents
of regret, yet unblessed by
the son who died, two daughters
now grown, all we couldn't know held
here in the rise and the fall of my breath –
and you, who left

The gold necklace you gave me
shoved to the back of a drawer, letters
we wrote, cards from a friend –
round pebbles moist in my thirsty mouth
their mineral taste rolls on my tongue; in the small
sweet weight of stones lies a measure
of grief, pleasures, pain, the small and the large
of what stays. We hold them
all, each child and each lover
in our skin forever.

WHAT TO TAKE

In the cabin, three clocks; two are still, one
ticks spasmodically. An arm lifts, falters, falls

set aside time

Grey light lifts off the lake. Rain puddles briefly
on leaves, slides off tree branches. Loud liquid
p*lops* on the sheet metal roof
nearby a horned owl's *hoo hoo*

use fewer words

The whole forest shines. On the wood steps,
slippery gleam. Last year's leaves
slide away from my feet, the lake's arms
open, whippoorwills call;
a beaver tail slaps, nose vees away.

jump in naked

When I leave, let me take
one last long breath

Travel lightly

ORANGES

Sky only blue and the light-fingered trees
Turn summer naked, autumn strips green away

Outside the cabin, goldenrod's bristled fur falls –
tea pot stands empty; the cracked cup will wait

On the path oak leaves silver-cloaked hoarfrost
stars grounded to glisten in morning's slow melt

Scarlet-crowned woodpecker's mad laughter wakes me
another old friend can't remember my name

My ancestors yearned after oranges
something to hope for, to imagine, to taste –

No light in here but the woodfire's flame
maybe that's why night has come

ON THE BACK OF AN ENVELOPE

How gravel and ice darkens
        to brittle patina

freezing rain, needled days
            become frosted nights

awake, I am only the grit
        of my dreams, uttered and falling

        past silence, the salt and sweet taste
            on my tongue
                of our spent days

                    indifferently mouthed

        in the numbed chill of my fingers
        sensation of loss

THE SMELL OF SNOW

Melting is

nose lifted
listen –
come sun touch
tongues warm
tincture of wet

remnants of drift
mettle of snowdrops
slight salt scent
cataclysmic

yearning
for petrichor

WINTER LETTER

Under a veil of slumbering trees, winter's day cracks
from beneath the sweet shell of darkness hardly
noticed by me, head bent by the fire
I am writing to you while
this house still sleeps,
and our good neighbours wake to
a home no longer theirs,
wonder what to take, what to leave,
where they will live
next month in this town where
renters have nowhere to go

I set letter aside,
pull on warm clothes, call the dog,
slide boots over socks, find dry mitts

My shovel hits snow: we must dig out

Winds sculpture drifts into rise of a hip,
deep folds of a belly, one long white leg
graceful lines
there's a goddess
                    asleep in my driveway

FROZEN

Created for springtime, my soul wants

walking dogs, joyful and leash-tugging
games of catch, balls thrown slow, lofted
to leather mitts, the waiting hands
of small children

seeds tucked in
to sharp-scented wet earth
peas, beans, radish, lettuce, rhubarb shoot
water and hoe, fork, edger, rake, trowel

But
this year the shoulder refuses
to lift hold embrace
whirl twirl in circles reach up
toward moons no waxing all wane

seized into throb cut of knife-blades
immovable

pain

frozen

Common, say doctors, in women–
years of strain   overreach
all I would carry
through so many seasons

now wintered in

VISIBILITY

after Kaveh Akbar, *Pilgrim Bell*

I don't invite
your judgement

I don't ask for
this body's frailties

You will never see me –

all I am
is much too large

to fit
inside your eye

A SPELL FOR THE ACHING

In the new-cracked egg of a just-born day,
black trees not yet green

light uncertain cloud swirls fill the sky with

dragon-tongue flames, royal purple-grey

pink burning sheen, tangerine taffeta swaths,
but words fail— enchanted, spell-bound

I am squalling,
  hungry, bewildered
    with wanting

this life –
its unspeakable ache

HAG DANCES

Hag
    an old woman

Hag
    the overhang at the edge of a cliff

Hagios
    from the Greek, meaning holy

Foot notes
    for edge-walking, way-finding

Choreography
    notes on the dance

Hag Dances: my Hageography

HAGEOGRAPHY

Black clouds
white-bearded waves
crash crest crash again
land-tossed storm-worn stones
rattle rock-lined shores, earth flesh falls away
swallowed

lake water
windlashed, cold not quite bitter
deep sturgeon green
eyes amber-flecked

open mouthed thunder unrolls bright bolts
this tongue of fire

as lightning seeks earth
old woman walks
home

ACKNOWLEDGEMENTS

I am a slow learner in the art and the craft of writing poetry. As a result, I have far more people to thank than I can possibly mention here.

A smattering:
My family and friends: you are many, which makes me a very fortunate human on this beloved and challenged planet. You make everything possible.

The land and the people of Wintergreen Studios have been a vibrant hub of sanctuary, community and creativity in my life for over ten years: Lorna Crozier, Rena Upitis, Monica Capovilla, the many staff and volunteers who make Wintergreen all that it is; my compatriots, the poets who gather there with me every year; poet friends Liz Huntly and Callista Markotich who coordinate twice-monthly online Wintergreen Poet gatherings.

The Writers' Union of Canada and League of Canadian Poets mentorship programs, where I created first drafts of this collection with Kyeren Regehr who, along with much else, taught me to love sonnets.

Dandelions: we met at Chelene Knight's Advanced Poetry Workshop, where I first imagined I might publish a poetry book or two and we have been together ever since—Karen Massey, Kimberly Peterson, Suzanne Doerge,

Mary Corkery, poetry nestmates ready to read my rawest, newest, least-likely-to-succeed.

Hen's teeth: the local poet friends scattered through Simcoe, Grey-Bruce, Dufferin counties and beyond. I am much less lonely, just knowing you are out here.

Sage Hills Writing, the wide prairie skies and my mentors Sandra Ridley and Sky Dancer Louise Bernice Halfe, the poets and writers I have met there and the wonderful staff who create a welcoming haven for writers.

Editors and readers at poetry journals, those who declined and those who accepted earlier versions of poems included here. Your efforts are invaluable in giving poets a chance to share our work.

Wintergreen Studios Press, which bravely took on the task of publishing the chapbook of visual images and poems that became Hand Shadows. Dancetheatre David Earle for everything I know about contemporary dance; Michele Green and Suzette Sherman who conceived the collaboration that inspired our performances and chapbook.

At Bay Press which somehow survives all the slings and arrows of independent Canadian publishing to carry on publishing poetry. Thanks, Matt for the whole adventure, including the invaluable editorial eye of Karen Clavelle.

If you are a person who reads all the way to Acknowledgements in books like this, you too are among the many people who have supported me in reaching the final pages of this book.

Thank you, all.

SUSAN WISMER is a queer poet who is grateful to live on Treaty 18 territory at the southern shore of Manidoo gitchigami (Georgian Bay) in Ontario, Canada with two human partners and a very large dog. Recent publications include *Hand Shadows, a chapbook* (Wintergreen Press, 2024) co-authored with Michele Green and Suzette Sherman. *Hag Dances* is her first full length collection.

OUR AT BAY PRESS ARTISTIC COMMUNITY

Publisher – Matt Joudrey
Managing Editor – Alana Brooker
Substantive Editor and Copy Editor – Karen Clavelle
Graphic Designer – Lucas c Pauls
Layout – Lucas c Pauls and Matt Joudrey
Publicity and Marketing – Savita Singh

Thanks for purchasing this book
and for supporting authors and artists.
As a token of gratitude,
please scan the QR code for
exclusive content from this title.

Forthcoming Titles From At Bay Press

MAN IN THE SHADOWS
Gordon Henderson

September 25, 2025

$24.95

Paperback
FICTION
9781998779901

MARY AND HER MÉTIS GRANDMA
Rita Jasper

November 12, 2025

$24.95

Paperback
FICTION
9781998779895

HUNTING HISTORY A WRITER'S ODYSSEY
Erna Paris

September 12, 2025

$34.95

Hardcover
BIOGRAPHY & AUTOBIOGRAPHY
9781998779888

ONLY THE SCENT OF YOU REMAINED
Duncan Mercredi

November 06, 2025

$24.95

Paperback
POETRY
9781998779871

HOW ABOUT THIS...?
Michael Mirolla

November 27, 2025

$24.95

Paperback
FICTION
9781998779864

CITY RISING: THE AGE OF DRY WATER
The Shanghai Tetralogy Book 4
David Rotenberg

September 23, 2025

$24.95

Paperback
FICTION
9781998779857

APRIL SNOW
Olivia Van Guinn

November 26, 2025

$24.95

Paperback
FICTION
9781998779840

SCREAMING AT OBSCENITIES THE SKY
Christian McPherson

November 27, 2025

$26.95

Paperback
COMICS & GRAPHIC NOVELS
9781998779833